Huntington County Board of County Commissioners

Historical sketch of Huntington County, Indiana

Huntington County Board of County Commissioners

Historical sketch of Huntington County, Indiana

ISBN/EAN: 9783337305543

Printed in Europe, USA, Canada, Australia, Japan

Cover: Foto ©ninafisch / pixelio.de

More available books at **www.hansebooks.com**

— OF —

HUNTINGTON COUNTY,

INDIANA.

HUNTINGTON, IND.
HERALD PRINTING COMPANY, PRINTERS
1 – 7 7 .

PREFACE.

---o---

RESOLUTION BY CONGRESS.

Be it resolved by the Senate and House of Representatives of the United States of America, in Congress assembled, That it be, and is hereby, recommended by the Senate and House of Representatives to the people of the several States that they assemble in their several counties or towns on the approaching Centennial Anniversary of our National Independence, and that they cause to have delivered on such day an historical sketch of said county or town from its formation, and that a copy of said sketch may be filed, in print or manuscript, in the Clerk's office of said county, and an additional copy, in print or manuscript, be filed in the office of the Librarian of Congress, to the intent that a complete record may thus be obtained of the progress of our institutions during the First Centennial of their existence.

Approved, March 13, 1876.

PROCLAMATION BY THE PRESIDENT.

Whereas a Joint Resolution of the Senate and House of Representatives of the United States was duly approved on the 13th day of March, last, which resolution is as follows:

"Be it resolved by the Senate and House of Representatives of the United States, in Congress assembled, that it be, and is hereby, recommended by the Senate and House of Representatives to the people of the several States that they assemble in their several counties or towns on the approaching Centennial Anniversary of our National Independence, and that they cause to have delivered on such day an historical sketch of said county or town from its formation, and that a copy of said sketch may be filed, in print or manuscript, in the Clerk's office of said county, and an additional copy, in print or manuscript, be filed in the office of the Librarian of Congress, to the intent that a complete record may thus be obtained of the progress of our institutions during the first Centennial of their existence."

And whereas it is deemed proper that such recommendation be brought to the notice and knowledge of the people of the United States:

Now, therefore, I, Ulysses S. Grant, President of the United States, do hereby declare and make known the same, in the hope that the object of such resolution may meet the approval of the people of the United States, and that proper steps may be taken to carry the same into effect.

Given under my hand at the City of Washington, the twenty-fifth day of May, in the year of our Lord one thousand eight hundred and seventy-six, and of the Independence of the United States the one hundredth.

[SEAL.]

U. S. GRANT.

By the President:

HAMILTON FISH, Secretary of State.

PROCLAMATION BY THE GOVERNOR OF INDIANA.

THE STATE OF INDIANA, }
EXECUTIVE DEPARTMENT. }

To the People of Indiana :

It having been recommended by the Senate and House of Representatives, in Congress assembled, by a joint resolution, approved March 13, 1876, that the people of the several States assemble in their several counties on the approaching Centennial Anniversary of our National Independence and cause to have delivered on such day an historical sketch of said county from its formation, and that a copy of the same, in print or manuscript, be filed in the office of the Clerk of said county, and that an additional copy, in print or manuscript, be filed in the office of the Librarian of Congress to the intent that a complete record may thus be obtained of the progress of our institutions during the first centennial of their existence ; and the President of the United States, by his proclamation of May 25, 1876, having added thereto his further recommendation of the same :

I, Thomas A. Hendricks, Governor of the State of Indiana, do hereby heartily concur in said recommendation, and commend the proper observance of said occasion to the people of our State.

Given under my hand and the seal of the State, at the City of Indianapolis, this 1st day of June, A. D. 1876, and of [SEAL.] the State the 60th.

THOMAS A. HENDRICKS,
Governor of Indiana.

Be the Governor :

JNO. E. NEFF, Secretary of State.

Pursuant to the above Proclamation, the Board of Commissioners of Huntington County, State of Indiana, appointed the following named citizens a Committee to make such preliminary arrangements as may be necessary to comply with the above recommendation, viz. : John Roche, James R. Slack, L. P. Milligan, H. B. Sayler and James Baldwin.

REPORT OF THE COMMITTEE.

To the Board of County Commissioners :

Your Committee to prepare an Historical Sketch of Huntington County present to you the result of their labors. They are conscious of its many defects, but express the hope that the facts narrated will be found to be interesting and valuable.

They acknowledge their obligations, for valuable assistance, to the following gentlemen : Capt. John Swaidner, John Hackett and Josiah S. Grim. of Jackson Township: Jacob Stults. Samuel M:Caughey and Joseph Wagner, of Clearcreek Township : Nehemiah Brown, J. H. Howenstine and John Stults, of Warren Township ; Samuel Copeland, Henry Kantz and F. M. Cole, of Dallas Township ; Thomas Roche, John Kenower and Sexton Emley, of Huntington Township ; John J. Anson, William O. Jones and James Thompson, of Union Township ; Dr. Joseph Scott, Jonathan Whitelock and John J. Scotten. of Rockcreek Township ; George Buzzard, David Heiney and Enos Boyd, of Lancaster Township : John C. Hart, M. McFarland and Charles E. Satterthwaite, of Polk Township ; George W. Leverton, Thomas Fisher and John Ruggles, of Wayne Township ; Oliver W. Sänger, Samuel Marshall and Peter Wire, of Jefferson Township ; Samuel H. Swaim, Leander Morrison and Robert Sprowl, of Salamony Township ; the Treasurer and Clerk of the City of Huntington ; the County Officers, and particularly William G. Bratton, Deputy Auditor, and Willis A. Jones, Deputy Clerk. whose assistance was peculiarly valuable.

> JOHN ROCHE,
> JAMES R. SLACK,
> L. P. MILLIGAN,
> H. B. SAYLER,
> JAS. BALDWIN,
> *Committee.*

INDEX.

———o———

HISTORICAL SKETCH

— OF —

HUNTINGTON COUNTY,

INDIANA.

The present territory of Huntington county, Indiana, is embraced within Townships 26, 27, 28 and 29 north, and four miles of range eight and ranges nine and ten east of the second principal meridian; it being three hundred and eighty-four square miles in extent.

It was first settled about the middle of August, 1828, by Artemus D. Woodworth, on section fourteen, in Dallas township. Soon afterwards, certainly not later than very early in 1830, Captain Elias Murray settled at the "Bluffs," near Woodworth's. In 1831, Joel Helvey and Champion Helvey settled on a part of the plat of the city of Huntington. In 1832, Albert Draper, a young man from Vermont, settled in Rockcreek township, near the mouth of Rock Creek. In 1833, the first settlement was made on the Salamony River, Samuel Jones being the first settler. In 1834, considerable settlements were made in different parts of the county, but emigration was slow until 1841, from which time the substantial development of the county dates.

Marcia Murray was the first white child born within the present limits of the county, that event occurring at the " Bluffs," in Dallas township, early in 1830. She was a daughter of Captain Elias and Henrietta Murray. Bridget Kennedy, a daughter of Michael and Mary Kennedy, was born in Huntington on the 11th day of March, 1834. Her mother, now Mrs. Sexton, still survives, and resides in the city of Huntington. Mary Jane McGrew, daughter of Noah and Elizabeth McGrew was born in Salamony township on the 5th day of April, 1834.

The first wedding in the county was that of Champion Helvey to Mary Barrett, which occurred in May, 1834, and was solemnized by Judge Everetts. In the fall of 1835, John E. George and Ann M. Murray were married. On the 26th day of February, 1835, Leander Morrison and Matilda Jones were married in Salamony township. During the same year, Albert Draper and Rachael Sparks were married in Rockcreek township ; Joseph Cheselbro and Susan C. Woodworth were married in Dallas township, and ————— Johnson and Sarah Keller, a daughter of Judge Keller, were married in Huntington township.

The first death of a white settler was that of the wife of William Delvin, of Huntington township, which occurred in 1832 or 1833.

The United States erected, on Rock Creek, in Rockcreek township, in 1832, the first saw-mill in the county, for the use of the Miami Indians ; and in 1835 a grist mill was built near the saw-mill by the Government, for the same purpose. In 1834, Daniel Johnson built a saw-mill one mile east of the city of Huntington. During the year 1835, flour mills were erected by Fleming Mitchell on the Salamony River, near Warren, and by William G. Johnson, on Cherry street, in the then town of Huntington.

John McGrew taught the first school in the county, about one mile below the town of Warren, on the Salamony River, in the year 1834. About the same time William Delvin taught a school in the town of Huntington, in a house a little west of the " American House."

Huntington county was organized on the 5th day of May, 1834, and then comprised the territory now embraced in Huntington, Wabash and Whitley counties. John Burke, Stearns Fisher and Lewis Rogers were the first County Commissioners; Champion Helvey was the first Sheriff; William S. Edsall was the first Clerk; Captain Elias Murray was the first County Treasurer, and Amos Harris was the first County Assessor. At that time the territory included in the present limits of this county was known as Huntington township.

The first term of the Circuit Court began on the 5th day of May, 1834, and was held by Gustavus A. Everetts, President Judge, and Jonathan Keller and Murdoch McLean, Associate Judges.

The present limits of the county were fixed early in 1835.

The first election was held at the house of Jonathan Keller, on the first Monday in June, 1834, to elect two Justices of the Peace for Huntington township. The next election was held in August of the same year. One hundred and forty-seven votes were polled at that election in the then Huntington township. Of those who voted at that time, Samuel Moore and Patrick Johnson are the only ones who still reside in the present limits of Huntington township.

At the second meeting of the Board of County Commissioners, on the 23th day of August, 1834, Charles G. Vorhees was appointed County Agent. At the same meeting the letting of a " public jail " was ordered to be advertised ; and Amos Harris was allowed fifteen dollars for assessing the county.

The first Coroner's jury was called to sit on the body of Thomas Riley, and was composed of the following persons : Jerry Todhunter, Champion Helvey, Obediah Ward, William Walker, Solomon Stout, Benjamin Sams, A. C. Evans, Paul Burk, Henry Drum, T. J. Lewis, Garrett Buckingham and Robert Wilson.

In 1835, Captain Elias Murray, County Treasurer, was allowed four dollars and fifty-one cents for collecting the taxes for the preceding year.

William Delvin was appointed County Collector for the year 1835.

The first Grand Jury sat in August, 1835, and was composed of the following persons: Elias Murray, Joel Grover, John F. Merrill, John Burk, Paul Burk, Thomas Brackenridge, George A. Fate, Obediah Ward, John Thompson, Channing Madison, Edwin Madison, William Delvin, Richard Adams, John Emley, James Delvin, Obediah Brown, Samuel Jones and Louis Purviance.

The Petit Jury for the same term of Court was composed of the following persons :   Jeremiah Barcus, William Walker, Sr., Champion Helvey, Joel Helvey, Jesse Griffith, Henry Miller, Eden Brown, Patrick Johnson, Hugh McCowen, Hugh O'Neal, Daniel Johnson, John E. George, David Kite, Albert Draper, Alexander McLane, Joseph Watson, Levi Turner, Stephen Chapman, Simon Cochrane, Edward Wall, Harrison Wall, Harrison Warner, James Gilleece, Thomas Delvin, Robert Wilson and George Turner.

On the 5th day of May, 1835, the Board of Commissioners allowed W. G. Johnson seventy dollars in full for his services as Sheriff to that date.

In February, 1838, Isaac N. Harlan was allowed eight dollars for making out the assessment roll of 1837.

In 1838, Charles W. Ewing was the President Judge of the Circuit Court, and Jonathan Keller and Murdock McLean were the Associate Judges.

Samuel W. Hawley was County Treasurer in 1836 and a part of 1837.

Joel Helvey was County Treasurer for part of 1837 and 1838, and Henry Bowles was Treasurer in 1839, 1840 and 1841.

John Burk, Paul Burk and John S. Merrill were the County Commissioners in 1834 and 1835.

William S. Edsall was clerk in 1834, 1835 and 1836, and Isaac N. Harlan was Clerk in 1837 and 1838.

Channing Madison, Rufus Adams and Peter Wire were County Commissioners in 1836.

On the 15th day of May, 1837, a Board of Justices was elected, consisting of Jesse Cleveland, John S. Merrill and Leander Morrison, who had charge of the county business. They continued in office until in the next year, when Samuel Moore was elected as the successor of John S. Merrill.

William Shearer was elected Clerk and R. H. Eddy was elected Sheriff. In 1839 and 1840, Henry Chase was Circuit Judge and Joseph Wiley, J. R. Emley and Nathan Fisher were the County Commissioners, which office had been re-established in the place of the Board of Justices.

In 1841 and 1842 John W. Wright was the Circuit Judge : Nathan Fisher, Alward White and John Leyman were the County Commissioners ; Chelsea Crandall was elected Sheriff and Joseph Wiley was elected Clerk, to which office he was re-elected from time to time, until 1854.

In 1843, James W. Borden was the Circuit Judge ; Alward White, Samuel H. Purviance and John Leyman were the County Commissioners ; James R. Slack was elected Auditor, Chelsea Crandall, Sheriff, and John Roche, Treasurer. James R. Slack was the first Auditor of the county.

In 1844, the same persons were county officers as in 1843, except James C. Best, who was elected a County Commsssioner as the successor of Alward White.

In 1845. James W. Borden was Circuit Judge; James C. Best, James Taylor and Samuel H. Purviance were the County Commissioners, James R. Slack, Auditor, John Buchanan, Sheriff, and Wilson B. Loughridge, Treasurer.

In 1846, the same persons were county officers as in 1845, except Nathan Fisher, who was elected a County Commissioner, as the successor of Samuel H. Purviance.

In 1847–48–49 and '50, the same persons were county officers as in 1845, except Sheriff, Chelsea Crandall having been elected in 1846 to succeed John Buchanan ; and in 1848 John Buchanan was elected to succeed Chelsea Crandall, and was re-elected in 1850, and the County Commissioners, who were as follows :   In 1847 and '48, James Taylor, Nathan Fisher and J. R. Emley ; in 1849 and '50, James Taylor, Albert Draper and Peter Emery.

In 1851, E. A. McMahon was Circuit Judge, and continued until February, 1853. Peter Emery, John Heiney and Albert Draper were County Commissioners ; John Alexander, Auditor ; John Buchanan, Sheriff ; and Samuel W. Hawley, Treasurer.

In 1852 the same persons were county officers as in 1851, except Hugh Montgomery, who was elected County Commissioner as the successor of Albert Draper.

In 1853, John U. Pettit was Circuit Judge, and continued until February, 1855. John Heiney, Hugh Montgomery and Sexton Emley were County Commissioners ; John Alexander, Auditor ; Samuel W. Hawley, Treasurer, and Henry Brown, Sheriff.

In 1854, Hugh Montgomery, Sexton Emley and John Alexander, of Salamony township, were County Commissioners ; Marshall J. Purviance was elected Treasurer, and Samuel H.

Purviance, Clerk. Martin B. Brandt was elected Recorder; he was the first Recorder elected by the people.

In 1855, John M. Wallace was Circuit Judge, and continued until March, 1861; John Alexander was re-elected Auditor, and John Kenower was elected County Commissioner, as the successor of Hugh Montgomery.

In 1856, Samuel McCaughey was elected Treasurer; James Taylor, County Commissioner, as the successor of John Alexander; Jacob Young, Sheriff, and John Roche, County Surveyor.

In 1857 the same persons were county officers as in 1856.

In 1858, Joseph Wiley was elected Clerk; Samuel McCaughey, Treasurer; and Samuel Emley, County Commissioner.

In 1859, John Carll was elected Auditor, and Enos Boyd County Commissioner.

In 1860, Oliver W. Sanger was elected Treasurer; Samuel Dougherty, Sheriff, and John Miller, County Commissioner.

In 1861, Horace P. Biddle was Circuit Judge, and continued until September, 1869. William O. Jones was elected County Commissioner.

In 1862, John Morgan was elected Clerk; John D. Jones, Treasurer; Frederick P. Lucas, Recorder; Luther Cummings, Sheriff; Andrew Wiley and George Keefer, County Commissioners; and Thomas Bolinger, County Surveyor.

In 1863, Martin B. Brandt was elected Auditor, and John Miller, County Commissioner.

In 1864, Jacob Mishler was elected Treasurer; Luther Cummings, Sheriff; Samuel Emley, County Commissioner; and William G. Bratton, County Surveyor.

In 1865, Enos Boyd was elected County Commissioner.

In 1866, John Morgan was elected Clerk; Jacob Mishler, Treasurer; Charles Mayne, Sheriff; Frederick P. Lucas, Recorder; and John Brubaker, County Commissioner.

In 1867, Reuben C. Ebersole was elected Auditor and Samuel Emley, County Commissioner.

In 1868, Joseph W. Purviance was elected Treasurer ; Charles Mayne, Sheriff; and Martin W. Little, County Commissioner.

In 1870, Thomas L. Lucas was elected Clerk ; Robert Simonton, Auditor; Joseph W. Purviance, Treasurer ; Aaron McKimmey, Sheriff; Isaac K. Schlosser, Recorder; and Daniel Kitch, John W. Baker and Oliver H. Fisher, County Commissioners.

In 1872, Sexton Emley was elected Treasurer ; Aaron McKimmey, Sheriff; Daniel Kitch and John W. Baker, County Commissioners, and James M. Hatfield, County Surveyor.

In 1873, John U. Pettit was Circuit Judge one term, when James R. Slack was appointed, and is Circuit Judge at this date.

In 1874, Thomas L. Lucas was elected Clerk ; Harvey C. Black, Auditor; Sexton Emley, Treasurer ; Aden J. Wiles, Sheriff; Lewis J. Day, Recorder; James W. Gusman, Surveyor ; and Oliver H. Fisher, County Commissioner.

In 1876, Daniel Christian was elected Treasurer ; Aden J. Wiles, Sheriff; James W. Gusman, Suryeyor ; and Joseph Wagoner, George Buzzard and Henry Heaston, Commissioners.

From 1844 to the present, the following persons have been Coroner of the county in the order named : David Myers, Isaac K. Schlosser, Joachim Fernandez, Luzon Warner, Joachim Fernandez, Tipton Allman and Granville Bocock.

The office of Common Pleas Judge was established in 1852. Wilson B. Loughridge was elected to that office in 1852, and re-elected in 1856, holding the office until 1860, in which year Joseph Breckenridge was elected, and held the office until 1864. James W. Borden was elected in 1864, and continued in the office until 1867, when he resigned, and Robert S. Taylor was appointed to fill the vacancy and held the office until 1868, when David Studabaker was elected. He resigned in 1869, and Robert S. Taylor was again appointed. In 1870, William W.

Carson was elected to fill the vacancy occasioned by the resignation of David Studabaker, and held the office until 1872, when Samuel E. Sinclair was elected, and continued in office until the office was abolished in 1873.

The following named persons were either elected or appointed Prosecuting Attorney in the Circuit Court for the following times, to wit:

Samuel C. Sample, March Term, 1835, to August Term, 1836.

Joseph L. Jernegan, August Term, 1836.

Thomas Johnson, March Term, 1837, to the March Term, 1839.

John W. Wright, March Term, 1839, to the March Term, 1840.

Lucinus P. Ferry, March Term, 1840, to the March Term, 1842.

William H. Coombs, March Term, 1842, to the September Term, 1843.

Lysander C. Jacoby, September Term, 1843, to the March Term, 1845.

Elza A. McMahon, March Term, 1845, to the March Term, 1848.

John S. Hendryx, March Term, 1848, to the September Term, 1849.

John R. Coffroth, September Term, 1849, to the April Term, 1851.

Elza A. McMahon, April Term, 1851.

Isaac DeLong, September Term, 1851.

Charles Case, March Term, 1852.

James L. Worden, September Term, 1852.

John M. Coombs, February Term, 1853.

William Potter, August Term, 1853.

Isaiah M. Harlan, February Term, 1854, to the February Term, 1855.

Lambdin P. Milligan, February Term, 1855, to the February Term, 1856.

Isaac DeLong, February Term, 1856.

Oris Blake, August Term, 1856, to the August Term, 1857.

Charles H. Parish, August Term, 1857, to the August Term, 1858.

Samuel Mahon, August Term, 1858.

Richard P. DeHart, March Term, 1859, to the September Term, 1860.

Henry B. Sayler, September Term, 1860.

M. H. Kidd, March Term, 1861, to the February Term, 1862.

Henry B. Sayler, February Term, 1862.

Thomas C. Whiteside, February Term, 1863, to the August Term, 1864.

Henry B. Sayler, August Term, 1864.

Dudley H. Chase, April Term, 1865, to the April Term, 1866.

Thomas Roche, April Term, 1866.

James C. Branyan, October Term, 1866.

George W. Stults, November Term, 1868.

Joseph S. Daily, September Term, 1869, to the March Term, 1873.

Alexander Hess, March Term, 1873.

William H. Carroll, June Term, 1873, to the December Term, 1873.

Alfred Moore, December Term, 1873, to the present time.

The following named persons were either elected or appointed Prosecuting Attorney in the Common Pleas Court for the following times, to wit:

John R. Coffroth, November Term, 1852.

Benedict Burns, April Term, 1853.

Lambdin P. Milligan, July Term, 1853.

John R. Coffroth, October Term, 1853, to the July Term, 1854.

Isaac DeLong, July Term, 1854, to the January Term, 1855.

Lambdin P. Milligan, January Term, 1855, to the October Term, 1855.

William C. Kocher, October Term, 1855, to the June Term, 1856.

John R. Coffroth, June Term, 1856, to the January Term, 1857.

Samuel Mahon, January Term, 1857, to the June Term, 1859.

Frederick P. Lucas, June Term, 1859, to March Term, 1860.

Newton Burwell, March Term, 1860, to the January Term, 1861.

David T. Smith, January Term, 1861, to the February Term, 1863.

David Colerick, February Term, 1863, to the February Term, 1867.

Joseph S. Daily, February Term, 1867, to the February Term, 1869.

Benjamin F. Ibach, February Term, 1869, to the February, Term, 1873.

A. H. Bittenger, February Term, 1873, which was the last Term of said Court, it having been abolished at that time by the Legislature.

The office of County Examiner of Common Schools was created in 1865. Richard A. Curran was appointed to this office in June, 1865, and continued in office until June, 1871, when Morris L. Spencer was appointed. He resigned in March, 1874, and in April following, Francis M. Huff was appointed, and still continues in office. In 1873 the designation of the office was changed, and is now known as "County Superintendent."

JACKSON TOWNSHIP.

Jackson Township was organized at the September term, 1841, of the Board of County Commissioners. The first election was at the house of Samuel Gettis. Andrew Boggs was the Inspector of the election. The township was first settled by Jared Darrow, who emigrated west with his family, consisting of four persons, from Rochester, New York, in the year 1837. He settled one mile south of the town of Roanoke. His nationality was American.

Within the next year Messrs. Thompson, Southwick, Decker, R. L. Eskridge and Paul H. Salts settled in the township. Paul H. Salts is the only one of these pioneers left surviving.

Captain Columbia built the first house in the township, which was built at Roanoke, and the first log-rolling was on the land of Lemuel G. Jones, near the lock at Roanoke. Lemuel J. Salts was the first white child born in the township. He was born in 1839. His parents were Paul H. and Lucy J. Salts.

The first marriage was in 1838, Joseph Satel and Sarah Darrow being the contracting parties.

The first death in the township was that of Francis Dupee, which occurred in 1841.

In 1845, L. G. Jones built the first saw-mill in the township at Roanoke. He also, in 1847, built the first flouring mill, near the Lock, then known as Dickey's Lock. At this time there are eight saw-mills and one flouring mill in the township.

The first school was kept at Wesley Chapel, two miles north of Roanoke, by William Allen. The first school-house was built at Wesley Chapel. Wesley Chapel was built in 1850 by the Methodist church. It was the first church built in the township.

Other denominations built churches in the following order: United Brethren, at Roanoke; Lutheran Church; United Brethren, at Brandenburg's; Zion United Brethren Church, on Bull Creek; New Lutheran and Catholic. The leading denominations are the United Brethren and Methodist.

Roanoke is a considerable town, representing many of the industries, and improving. It has a population of about 1,000.

————o————

CLEARCREEK TOWNSHIP.

Clearcreek Township was organized on the 24th day of February, 1838. It was six miles wide, north and south, and sixteen miles long. The first election was held on the first Monday in April, 1838, at the house of John R. Emley. Thomas Delvin was the first township clerk.

The township was reduced in September, 1841, by the organization of Jackson township. It was again reduced, and to its present limits, in June, 1843, by the organization of Warren township.

The township was first settled by Michael Doyle, who located on the southeast quarter of section thirty-three, in the fall of 1834. He built the first log cabin in the township, a portion of the back wall of which still marks its site. The present owner of the premises, Daniel Kitch, has planted this year a Centennial tree where the "old house" stood, to preserve the identity of its location.

Michael Doyle had five persons in his family. His nationality was Irish. Within the next year John R. Emley, with his wife and nine children, settled on the northeast quarter of section twenty-nine. Eight of his children still survive.

James McCambridge and his brother also settled in the township late in 1834.

The first log-rolling was on the farm of Thomas Delvin, in section thirty-three, in 1835.

Elizabeth Miller was the first white child born in the township. She was the daughter of Henry Miller, and was born in May, 1836.

The first wedding occurred in November, 1841, Samuel Reams and Louisa Dial being the principal parties in the ceremony.

The first death was that of Wesley Emley, which occurred in October, 1836.

In 1836, John R. Emley erected a corn mill, the first in "all that region." In 1843, Samuel C. Emley built the first sawmill on section twenty-eight. At this time there are five sawmills in operation in the township.

Abraham Binkley "kept" the first school in the township, at Emley's school-house, which stood near the present site of Clearcreek Church, but which has long since disappeared.

The first school-house was built in 1838, on the northeast quarter of section twenty-nine, and was known as the Emley school-house.

The first church was built in the centre of the township by the United Brethren. Denominations followed and organized in the following order: Christian, Evangelists, Methodist and German Baptist.

The German Baptist, United Brethren and Methodist are the leading denominations.

Anthony Emley, in 1835, carried the second lot of flour ever used in the township on his shoulder from Huntington, in two loads of one hundred pounds each.

The venerable Jacob Kitt, 96 years old, resides in this township. He is probably the oldest man in the county.

WARREN TOWNSHIP.

Warren Township was organized at the June Term, 1843, of the Board of County Commissioners. The first election was held at the school-house near John Altman's. Jacob Shull was the inspector of the election.

The township was first settled in 1835 by George Zellers, who moved with his family, consisting of eight persons, from Wayne County, Ohio, to section eleven. His nationality was German.

Within the next year, Thomas Staley and George Schlosser settled in the township. George Schlosser sowed the first wheat ever sowed in the township.

The first log-rolling was on the farm of George Zellers.

M—— Staley, the child of Thomas and Amanda Staley, was the first white child born in the township, which birth occurred in 1836.

The first marriage was that of William Delvin and Susan Zellers in 1837.

The first death was that of a man named Noyer, who was killed by the falling of a tree in 1841.

Joseph Miller built the first saw-mill in the township in 1856, on section twenty-two, and two years afterwards, on the same section, he erected the first flouring-mill. There are now four saw-mills and one shingle-mill in operation.

In 1841, John W. Funk taught the first school on section eleven. The first school-house was built in 1841, on section eleven, at "Altman's Corners."

In 1855 the Lutherans built the first church in the township. It was erected on section twenty-one. Following the Lutherans, the Methodist, United Brethren, German Baptist, Second Adventist and Disciple denominations organized in the order of time as above set out. The Lutherans and United Brethren are the leading denominations in the township.

Christian Daily, George France and John T. Cook were the first Trustees. William T. Guffin was the first Township Clerk. James White was the first Township Treasurer. John Altman was the first Justice of the Peace, and John W. Funk was the first Constable.

————o————

DALLAS TOWNSHIP.

Dallas Township was organized at the March Term, 1847, of the Board of County Commissioners. It was settled about the middle of August, 1828, by Artemus D. Woodworth, who with his family, consisting of five persons, settled on the northwest quarter of section fourteen. His nationality was American.

Capt. Elias Murray settled near by Woodworth's not long afterwards, certainly as early as the winter of 1829-30.

The first house was built, and the first log-rolling occurred on the farm of Artemus H. Woodworth.

Marcia Murray, a daughter of Capt. Elias and Henrietta Murray was the first white child born in the township. The exact date of her birth is unknown, but it was early in 1830.

On the 18th day of November, 1835, Joseph Cheesebro and Susan C. Woodworth were married. This was the first marriage in the township.

Artemus D. Woodworth and William G. Campbell erected the first saw-mill. It was built in 1833, on the west branch of Silver Creek, about one and a half miles from its junction with Wabash River. There are now five saw-mills in the township.

The first flouring-mill was built by Elijah Snowden, in 1862, in the town of Antioch.

The first school was "kept" in 1844 and 1845. Elizabeth H. Edwards was the first teacher. The school was taught in the house erected in 1844 as a "Meeting-house" and school-house, on the southeast quarter of section two, on a lot donated by John Moore to the Society of Friends for "Meeting-house and burial purposes." The house was used as a "Meeting-house" by the "Friends," and was the first house erected for church purposes in the township. Other churches were built in the following order: United Brethren, German Lutheran, Methodists, Christians and German Baptists.

Antioch is the only town in the township. It was laid out in 1853, and contains a population of about five hundred. The original proprietor was Abraham Leedy. Additions thereto have been platted by Jacob Wintrode, Doctor Campbell and Elijah Snowden. It has three churches, one fine brick school house, and various manufacturing and mercantile establishments, all indicating a prosperous and energetic population.

John Moore, the founder of the "Friends' Meeting" in the township, was one of the early pioneers, and was principally instrumental in securing the settlement of a considerable portion of the township by members of that Society at an early day. He was a native of North Carolina, and moved to Wayne county, Indiana, in 1825, and from thence to this township in 1837. He died in 1872, aged nearly eighty-four years.

HUNTINGTON TOWNSHIP.

Huntington Township was first reduced by the organization of Salamony Township on the 24th day of February, 1835 ; next by by the organization of Lancaster Township on the 15th day of May, 1837 ; and next by the organization of Clearcreek Township on the 24th day of February, 1838. These four townships were then each six miles wide, north and south, and sixteen miles long. Huntington Township was again reduced by the organization of Monroe Township, (now called Union,) at the September term, 1842, of the Board of County Commissioners, and finally to its present limits by the organization of Dallas Township at the March term, 1847, of the Board of County Commissioners.

The first settlers of the present limits of the township were Joel Helvey and Champion Helvey, who came in 1831, and settled on a part of the present plat of the City of Huntington. They moved here from the Wabash River, opposite the mouth of the Salamony River. They were natives of Tennessee.

The first house was built by the Helveys on the bank of Little River, near the mouth of Flint Creek, which was used as a tavern, and was known as Flint Springs Hotel. The first log-rolling was on what is known as the Chief's farm, at the forks of the Wabash River.

Bridget Kennedy, a daughter of Michael and Mary Kennedy, was the first white child born in the township. She was born on the 11th day of March, 1834.

The first marriage was that of Champion Helvey to Mary Barrett, which occurred in May, 1834, and was solemnized by Judge Everetts. John E. George and Ann M. Murray were married in the fall of 1834. —— Johnson and Sarah Keller, a dauhgter of Judge Keller, were married in 1835. In the spring of 1837 Samuel Moore and Mary A. Fóxtater were married. This is the first marriage in the county of which any public record is found.

The first death was that of the wife of William Delvin. She died in 1832 or 1833.

The first saw-mill was built in 1834 by Daniel Johnson, one mile east of the City of Huntington. There are now seven sawmills in operation in the township.

In 1837 William G. Johnson built the first flouring-mill. It was erected on the south bank of Flint Creek, on Cherry street, in the City of Huntington. There are now four flouring-mills in the township.

The first school was kept in the house of Jonathan Keller, a few feet west of the present site of the American House, in the City of Huntington, in the winter of 1834 and 1835, and was taught by William Delvin. The first school-house was built on the south side of Market street, on a lot three lots west of the American House, and school was kept in the house in the winter of 1835 and 1836. The teacher's name was McClure. The house was also used as a Court House.

The first Church was built by the Roman Catholic denomination on out-lot No. 1. Other denominations organized in the following order: Baptist, Methodist, Presbyterian, Lutheran, Christian, German Reformed and United Brethren. The leading denomination is the Roman Catholic.

The only town in the township is the City of Huntington. The original proprietor was Gen. John Tipton, of Logansport. The original lots were sold by Capt. Elias Murray, the attorney of Gen. Tipton. A more extended notice of the city will be given at a subsequent page.

UNION TOWNSHIP.

Union Township was first organized at the September term, 1842, of the Board of County Commissioners, and named "Monroe Township." At the June term, 1845, the township was re-organized, and called Union Township.

It was first settled in 1836, by John McEwen, who settled on section thirty-two. There were three persons in his family. John A. Freel and John Lewis settled in the township within the next year.

The first house was built and the first log-rolling took place on the farm of John McEwen.

The first white child born in the township was John Barnes.

The first death was that of Christian Wolf.

Andrew Brandstrater, in 1847, built the first saw-mill. It was built on Flat Creek. There are three saw-mills now in operation in the township.

Jacob Good kept the first school in the township, It was kept on section thirty.

The first school-house was built on section thirty-two.

The first church was built in 1870, all denominations joining in its erection. The only other church building in the township is the Allbright.

ROCKCREEK TOWNSHIP.

Rockcreek Township was organized at the September term, 1842, of the Board of County Commissioners.

The first election was held at the house of George Poff. William Clark was the Inspector. The ballot-box was a hat, and the whole number of votes cast was *twelve.*

The first settler was Albert Draper, a single man from Vermont, who came in 1832, and settled at the Indian Mills, on the Richardville Reserve. His nationality is American.

Mr. J. Tracy came 1833, and Moses Sparks in 1834.

Albert Draper still survives, and resides in Upper Alton, Illinois. He built the Indian Mills for the United States for the use of the Miami Indians. This was the first house built in the Township.

The first log-rolling was on the farm of Moses Sparks, in section twenty-four.

Riley Draper, a son of Albert and Rachel Draper, was born in 1836. He was the first white child born in the township, and the marriage of his parents, which occurred in 1835, was the first marriage.

The death of Mrs. Adams in August, 1838, was the first death in the township. Eliza First, the wife of Israel First, died in the same month.

The first saw-mill and flouring-mill were the Indian Mills, above referred to. There are in the township at the present time ten saw-mills and three flouring-mills.

The first school taught by Thomas O'Thigh, in 1839, on section three, on the farm now owned by Jonas Kelsey ; and the next year the first school-house was built on section thirty-one.

The first church was built in 1861 by the Missionary Baptists at Markle. Other denominations built churches in the following order: Presbyterians, Disciples and Methodists.

The town of Markle was laid out by J. Tracy, where he built a house in 1833, and kept a grocery store in the woods three miles from the nearest settler. It has a population of about 300.

At the first election Albert Draper was elected Justice of the Peace, John Sheets, Jacob F. Sours and N. Polson were elected Township Trustees, and William Clark was elected Township Clerk.

The Township was first divided into School Districts in 1842.

———o———

LANCASTER TOWNSHIP.

Lancaster Township was organized on the 15th day of May, 1837. Its territory was reduced by the organization of Rockcreek Township in September, 1842, and was again reduced, and to its present limits, by the organization of Polk Township in March, 1846.

The township was first settled in May, 1834, by Joseph Sprowl, who, with his family, consisting of ten persons, moved from Preble county, Ohio, and settled on section thirty-four. His nationality was American.

Joseph P. Anthony and Abram Nordyke came in February, 1835, and Solomon Shideler with his family, consisting of five persons, came in the fall of the same years. Joseph P. Anthony, Jacob Shideler, and James, Mary Ann, Elizabeth, Robert, W. M. and Davidson Sprowl still survive.

The first road district embraced Lancaster, Jefferson and Wayne Townships, and Abram Nordyke was the first Supervisor.

The first house was built and the first log-rolling occurred on Joseph Sprowl's farm, in section thirty-four.

The first marriage in the township was solemnized in November, 1837, Charles Morgan and Elizabeth Fisher being the contracting parties.

The first death was that of Mrs. Wolgarmoth, which occurred in April, 1837.

William Markes built the first saw-mill. It was built on Richland Creek, on section thirty-one, in 1843. The first flouring-mill was built in 1838, on the Salamony River, on section thirty, by Henry Hildebrand, Sr. At this time there are six saw-mills and two flouring-mills in the township.

The first school was kept in 1838, on the Charleston section, by Nancy Hildebrand. The first school-house was built in 1840, at Mt. Etna.

The first church was built in 1840, at Mt. Etna, by the Methodist Episcopal denomination. Other denominations organized in the following order: Christians, German Baptists, Wesleyan Methodists, United Brethren, Lutherans, Disciples and Church of God. The leading denominations are the German Baptist and Methodist Episcopal.

John Hefner was the original proprietor of Mt. Etna, a town of about 300 inhabitants. Solomon Shideler was the original proprietor of New Lancaster, a town of about 130 inhabitants, and James Crosby was the original proprietor of Kelso, a town of about 70 inhabitants.

POLK TOWNSHIP.

Polk Township was organized at the March Term, 1846, of the Board of County Commissioners. It was first settled on the 23d day of September, 1836, by Jacob Fisher, who, with his family, consisting of nine persons, moved from Clinton County, Ohio, and located on the northwest quarter of section twenty-four. He is a native of North Carolina.

Within the next year, Nathan Fisher, Willis Jeffrey, John Campbell, Leonard Parrott, Greenbury Martin, Daniel James and Daniel Webb settled in the township. All these pioneers still survive except Leonard Parrott.

The first house was built and the first log-rolling occurred on Willis Jeffrey's farm.

Silas B. Fisher, a son of Nathan and Elizabeth Fisher, who was born on the 11th day of December, 1836, was the first white child born in the township.

The first marriage took place in 1838, Charles Morgan and Elizabeth Fisher being the parties.

On the 3d day of November, 1842, Susannah Fisher died. She was a daughter of Jacob Fisher. This was the first death in the township.

The first saw-mill was built in the Spring of 1837, on Little Majenica, by John Campbell. He attached a "corn cracker" to the saw-mill. There are five saw-mills in operation at the present time. The first flouring-mill was built on the Salamonie River by Henry Hildebrand, Sr.

The first school was kept in a log cabin on the northeast corner of section twenty-five by Dr. Anderson. The first school-house was built in 1838, on the northeast corner of the northwest quarter of section twenty-five.

The first church was built in 1856, on the school section, by the Wesleyan Methodists. The Christians built the next church. The leading denomination is the Methodist Episcopal.

In the spring of 1874, Jacob Leedy and John Pilcher laid out the town of Monument City—so called because of a very elegant marble monument erected at that point by the people of the township in memory of the soldiers who entered the army in the late war from the township, who were killed or died of disease during the term of their enlistment.

————()————

WAYNE TOWNSHIP.

Wayne Township was organized at the June term, 1844, of the Board of County Commissioners. The name was suggested by Thomas Fisher, in honor of Wayne County, Indiana.

The first election was held at the house of Joseph Weavers. Henry Kline was the Inspector.

The township was first settled on the 8th day of March, 1835, by John Ruggles and his family, consisting of six persons, and John Buzzard and his family, consisting of nine persons. They moved from Ohio together. John Ruggles settled on the northeast quarter of section thirteen, and John Buzzard settled on the southeast quarter of section twelve. Their nationality was American. Within the next year, Anderson Leverton, Asher Fisher, Thomas Fisher, Thomas Hollowell and Jacob Snider settled in the township. John Ruggles, Asher Fisher and Thomas Fisher still survive.

The first house was built and the first log-rolling occurred on John Ruggles' farm.

The first white child born in the township was Wesley Buzzard, who was born on the 15th day of April, 1835. He was a son of John and Rachel Buzzard.

In 1837, Oliver W. Sanger married Catherine A. Snider. This was the first marriage in the township.

The first death was that of Ary Cecil, which occurred on the 8th day of April, 1839.

The first saw-mill was built by John Sparks. There are two saw-mills in operation in the township.

The first school was taught in John Buzzard's cabin by Nancy Hildebrand. The first school-house was built in 1839, on section twelve.

The first church was built by the Baptists in 1860, on section thirty-four. The leading denomination is the Baptist.

———o———

JEFFERSON TOWNSHIP.

Jefferson Township was organized at the March term, 1843, of the Board of County Commissioners. The first election was held at the house of William Purviance, of which election he was Inspector.

The township was first settled by George W. Helms in February, 1834, who, with his family, consisting of four persons, moved from Preble County, Ohio, and located on section twelve. His nationality was American. Peter Wire, with his family, consisting of four persons, moved into the township in October, 1834. Of these pioneers, Peter Wire, Newton Wire and M. F. Wire still survive.

The first house was built by George W. Helms on section twelve. The first log-rolling took place on Peter Wire's farm.

The first white child born in the township was Lavina Wire. She was the daughter of Peter and Nancy Wire, and was born on the 4th day of March, 1836.

In 1839, Frederick Hefner married Nancy Cook. This was the first marriage in the township.

The first death was that of Mr. Stewart, which occurred in August, 1838.

In 1839 or 1840, Aaron Bond and John Hefner built the first saw-mill. It was built on Richland Creek, on section six. At the same time and place the same persons built the first flouring-mill. At this time there are two saw-mills and one flouring-mill in the township.

In 1838 the first school-house was built. It was erected on section three. The first school was taught during the same year in the " new school-house " by David C. Little.

The first church was built in 1870 by the Christians, in section nine, and is known as Purviance Chapel. The Methodist Episcopal, United Brethren and Friends also have organizations in the township.

Samuel E. Satterthwaite is the proprietor of the town of Pleasant Plain, a village of about forty inhabitants.

SALAMONY TOWNSHIP.

Salamony Township was organized on the 24th day of February, 1835. Its original territorial extent was six miles wide, north and south, and sixteen miles east and west. It was the first division of the present limits of the county into townships. An election for the choice of a Justice of the Peace was held on the 6th day of April, 1835. Samuel Jones was appointed Inspector of the election.

The township was reduced to its present limits at the March term, 1843, of the Board of County Commissioners.

The first settlement was made on the 27th day of September, 1833, by Samuel Jones, a soldier in the war of 1812. He settled on the present site of the town of Warren. He, with his family, consisting of eight persons, moved from Highland County, Ohio. His nationality was American. Within the next year Fleming Mitchell, Lewis Richards, James Morrison. Leander Morrison, Andrew Beard, Noah McGrew, Ezra C. Thompson (who was one of the garrison of Fort Nisbit, Ohio), John McGrew, L. W. Purviance, Ezekiel Fleming, David Wire (a survivor of Sinclair's defeat) and Michael Revael settled within the present limits of the township. Of all this goodly company of pioneers, Mrs. Samuel Jones. Fleming Mitchell. Leander Morrison, Andrew Beard and John McGrew alone survive.

The first house was built by Samuel Jones, and the first log-rolling occurred on the present site of the town of Warren.

Mary Jane McGrew, a daughter of Noah and Elizabeth McGrew, was the first white child born in the township. She was born on the 5th day of April, 1834.

The first marriage was that of Leander Morrison and Matilda Jones, which occurred on the 26th day of February, 1835.

Michael Revael died on the 20th of January, 1835. This was the first death in the township.

Fleming Mitchell built the first saw-mill about one mile above Warren. He also built the first flouring-mill in 1835. Bolting was attached in 1837 by John Reid, who came from Massachusetts. At this time there are two saw-mills and three flouring-mills in operation in the township.

The first school was taught one mile below Warren by John McGrew, and the first school-house was built near the Mounds, south of Warren.

The first church was built in the town of Warren by the Reformed Presbyterians. Other denominations followed in the following order: Baptist, Methodist, Universalist, Christian and United Brethren. The leading denomination is the Methodist Episcopal.

The town of Warren is the only town in the township. It has a population of about 450.

THE CITY OF HUNTINGTON.

The town of Huntington was incorporated on the 16th day of February, 1848. Its population in 1850 was 594; in 1860 it was 1,664; in 1870 it was 2,925, and at the present time it is about 4,500. The town organized as a city on the 17th day of September, 1873.

The value of lots and improvements, as returned for taxation, is $677,540. The value of personal property, as returned for taxation, is $436,525 : making a total of $1,113,865. The actual value of the real and personal property of the city is not far from $2,500,000, making the average wealth of the population about $500 for each of its 4,500 people.

It has eight churches, all supporting regular pastors.

Its public schools have reached a very high degree of excellence, and are justly the pride of its citizens. The present organiza ion of the public schools has been in operation three years, with the most satisfactory results. The public school-house and grounds are substantial and elegant, and compare very favorably with any in the State. The school revenue of the City Schools for tuition for the year ending June 16th, 1876, amounted to $5,262.99, and for the Special Fund it amounted to $6,300.85. During the last year the school was in session 200 days. There were 1,267 school children in the city limits, and 579 were enrolled in the City Schools. The average attendance was 456. The cost of each pupil for the year was $11.40—a little more than five cents per day. The course of instruction, running through eleven years, is quite extensive, very fully preparing pupils to enter the highest colleges of the land, as well as to discharge the business and enjoy the delights of the intellectual pursuits of life. The schools are under the direction of Prof. James Baldwin, who has been Superintendent for three years, assisted by a corps of nine teachers. The following articles were prepared for and sent to the Centennial Exposition at Philadelphia: A geological cabinet, containing nearly four hundred specimens in mineralogy and geology, collected and arranged principally by the pupils of Grade B, Miss E. A. Collins, teacher ; a collection of the native woods of Huntington County (fifty-seven specimens), the work of the High School, Herman Heinrichs, teacher ; a volume of maps and pen drawings, executed by grades D, C and B, Mrs. M. A. McCaslin, Miss Alma Holman, Miss Kate Hunt and Miss E. A. Collins the teachers, respectively : four volumes of examination papers (prepared at the regular monthly examination in December), copies of reports, blanks, course of study, &c. This display attracted the attention and admiration of the public in that vast display of the achievements of the world. William McGrew, William Ewing and Alexander W. DeLorg are the Trustees.

In addition to the public schools, the German Reformed Church, the Lutheran Church and the Catholic Church each supports a school. The number enrolled in the German Reformed School is 50 : the average attendance is 45. During the last year the school was in session 190 days. The school is taught in the English and German language, and its course of instruction is substantially that of a common English education. The tuition per pupil is fifty cents per month. The value of the school property is about $3,000. The Rev. P. H. Dipple, the pastor of the church, is the teacher.

The number enrolled in the Lutheran School is 70 : the average attendance is 60. During the last year the school was in session 120 days. The school is taught in the German language, and its course of instruction is substantially that of a common English education. The Rev. A. Steger, the pastor of the church, is the teacher.

The number enrolled in the Catholic School is 235 ; the average attendance is 213. During the past year the school was in session 210 days. The expenses of the school aggregate $1,200 per annum, which is provided by the members of the church, making an average of about $5.70 per pupil. The school-house is an elegant building, three stories high, erected by members of the church, at a cost of $18,000. The advanced boys' classes are taught by John McCarthy ; the other classes are taught by four "Sisters of Notre Dame." The course of instruction prepares pupils to enter college.

The most prominent manufacturing establishments are Briant & Taylor's Stave Factory, operating 75 hands; Taylor & Griffith's Plow-handle Factory, operating 30 hands ; Drover's Spoke Factory, operationg 25 hands ; Moffitt & Roche's Foundry and Machine Shop, operating 15 hands; Niblock's Flax, Tow and Bagging Factory, operating 30 hands ; Townsend & Kenower's Lumber and Planing Mill, operating 19 hands ; Thorne, Slack & Ayres' Planing Mill, operating 14 hands ; A. Q. Kenower's Cabinet Factory, operating 12 hands ; Hall & Hendrix's Carriage Factory, operating 9 hands ; F. Kopp's Cabinet Factory, operating 7 hands ; 6 Boot and Shoe Establishments, operating 35 hands ; 4 Tailoring Establishments, operating 22 hands ; S. T. Morgan's Chair-stuff Mill, operating 6 hands ; Huntington Manufacturing Co., Irregular Wood Stuff, operating 4 hands; 2 Newspaper Offices, operating 8 hands ; 2 large Flouring Mills are in operation for merchant and custom work. There are many other establishments, giving constant employment to a large number of artizans. The mercantile portion of the community is large, representing every department of trade. The trade of the city is quite extensive, embracing, as it does in many departments, a territory of more than 400 square miles, and a population of more than 30,000. The Lime interest, which is very large and very important, has been referred to on another page. In short, Huntington is one of the most thriving and prosperous cities in the Wabash Valley.

————0————

AGRICULTURAL SOCIETY.

The first Agricultural Fair was held in the Old Court House, on the north-west corner of Jefferson and Franklin streets, in Huntington, in the fall of 1852, under the direction of John Becker, Albert Draper, Robert Fyson, Sr., James B. Custance, Jacob Snyder and others; but without definite organization. The articles on exhibition were principally Fruit, Vegetables and Needle Work.

On the 15th of December, 1852, a call was issued and published in the "Indiana Herald" for a meeting to be held on the first day of January, 1853, for the purpose of organizing an Agricultural Society. The call was signed by Wm. G. Sutton, D. Garlick and Warren Hecox, On the first day of January, 1853, a meeting was held with Jacob Snyder as Chairman, L. P. Milligan, Secretary, and Wm. G. Sutton, Treasurer, *pro tem.* After discussion of the subject, it was determined to permanently organize a Society, and the 5th day of February, 1853, was fixed for the election of Officers, at which time Charles H. Lewis was chosen President : Warren Hecox, Vice-President; Wm. Norton, Secretary; Wm. G. Sutton, Treasurer, and Albert Draper, James Purviance, Sexton Emley, Edward Coles, Thomas Moore, Jacob Snyder, David Chambers, James Miller, Thomas Fisher, Peter Weese, E. Flemming and Robert Fyson, Sr., Directors.

On the 7th of August, following, Charles H. Lewis resigned his office of President, and Warren Hecox became President. James Purviance, Robert Fyson, Sr., and Albert Draper prepared and submitted a list of Premiums, offering in the aggregate the sum of $99.75, which list was adopted by the Society.

The Society held its first Fair on the 18th and 19th days of October, 1853, on the south side of Little River, just below the old bridge, about where the residence of Samuel Buchanan now stands. The Fair was a success financially, its account showing $180.60 of receipts, and the expenditures, being for premiums, $67.75, miscellaneous $26.48, total $94.12, leaving a balance of $86.48 on hand.

On the 4th of February, 1854, John Becker was elected President, Robert Fyson, Sr., Vice-President, Wm. G. Sutton, Treasurer, and S. W. Hawley, Secretary. A Fair was held on the 17th and 18th days of October, of that year, in the eastern part of Huntington, in what is known as Orrin Brown's meadow.

On the 16th and 17th days of October, 1855, the Society held a Fair on the south side of Little River, just east of what was then known as Bratton's Grove. James M. Bratton was President and A. W. DeLong was Secretary. After this Fair the organization was abandoned.

A meeting was held on the 28th day of February, 1857, at which it was determined to re-organize the Society, and on the 7th of April following a temporary organization was effected, with Peter Weese, President ; L. P. Milligan, Vice-President ; A. M. Lewis, Secretary, and Wm. L. Steele, Treasurer.

A permanent organization was completed on the 6th of June, with the same Officers as above set out, except for Treasurer, to which office John Roche was elected, and the following Directors : James Leverton, Jacob Stults, John Becker, Robert Fyson, Sr., Peter Keefer, Thomas Fisher, Wm. B. Morgan, Thomas

Moore, John Miller, Joseph Miller and Lewis W. Purviance. No Fair was held this year.

On the 12th day of August, 1858, Jacob Stults was elected President; John Becker, Vice-President; A. M. Lewis, Secretary, and Wm. G. Sutton, Treasurer. At the same meeting a thorough canvass of the county, by a number of speakers and a company of singers, under the direction of Wm. L. Steele, was determined upon. Grounds just west of Huntington, on the north side and adjoining the Canal, had been secured by the Society, and a Fair was held on the 26th, 27th and 28th days of October, 1858. The Fair was a success.

On the 4th day of June, 1859, L. P. Milligan was elected President; Elijah Snowden, Vice-President; A. M. Lewis, Secretary, and Wm. G. Sutton, Treasurer.

The Society held its Fair this year on its grounds on the 28th, 29th and 30th days of September.

During the year 1860 Wm. Oden was President and Joseph Chesebro, Vice-President, A. M. Lewis, Secretary, and Jacob Snyder, Treasurer.

The Society held its Fair this year on its grounds on the 3d, 4th and 5th days of October.

The officers for 1861 were Dr. H. S. Heath, President; Robert Fyson, Sr., Vice-President; A. M. Lewis, Secretary, and Wm. Stults, Treasurer, and the Fair was held on the 25th, 26th and 27th days of September.

Dr. H. S. Heath was President in 1862; Silas Jones, Vice-President; A. M. Lewis, Secretary, and John Roche, Treasurer.

In December, 1863, Dr. H. S. Heath was elected President; L. P. Milligan, Vice-President; A. M. Lewis, Secretary, and Tipton Allman, Treasurer.

The Society struggled along until the 14th day of January, 1865, when the organization was abandoned. No Fairs had been held subsequent to 1861.

On the 4th day of January, 1868, a meeting was held at the Court House, in Huntington, to reorganize the Society, and Peter W. Zent was elected President; O. W. Sanger, Vice-President; John Roche, Treasurer, and Robert Simonton, Secretary.

The present grounds of the Society were secured and a Fair held in 1869, the same persons being the officers of the Society, they having been elected for this year.

The Society has held its Fairs regularly every year since that time.

The following were the officers of the Society from 1870 to the present:

For 1870—President, Peter W. Zent; Vice-President, Frank McKeever; Treasurer, Daniel Kitch; Secretary, Robert Simonton.

For 1871—President, P. W. Zent; Vice-President, Robert Fyson, Sr.; Treasurer, Daniel Kitch; Secretary, Robert Simonton.

For 1872—President, John D. Jones; Vice-President, H. F. Billiter; Treasurer, Daniel Kitch; Secretary, Robert Simonton.

For 1873—President, P. W. Zent; Vice-President, Frank McKeever; Treasurer, Daniel Kitch; Secretary, Alfred Moore.

For 1874—President, P. W. Zent; Vice-Presid't, Peter Weese; Treasurer, Daniel Kitch; Secretary, Alfred Moore.

For 1875—President, Luther Cummings; Vice-President, Frank McKeever; Treasurer, Daniel Kitch; Secretary, Robert Simonton.

For 1876—President, Frank McKeever; Vice-President, Jacob Stults; Treasurer, Daniel Kitch; Secretary, Robt. Simonton, who afterwards resigned and T. L. Lucas was elected his successor.

For 1877—President, Frank McKeever; Vice-President, Jacob Stults; Treasurer, Peter Weese; Secretary, Willis A. Jones.

The success of the Society has been very gratifying to its friends, and its influence in developing the resources of the County has been and is very marked. From the small beginning, noted above, it has grown to be a powerful corporation, involving in its transactions large and influential interests. Particular attention has been given to the improvement of hogs, and the result is that Huntington County is producing hogs, probably, superior in quality to those produced in any other locality in the United States. Like results would doubtless follow any other special effort of the Society. Its continued prosperity is of public importance.

HUNTINGTON COUNTY.

Huntington county was covered by a native forest equal to any, in this latitude, on the continent. Its hard woods are of a long, tough fibre, making them exceedingly valuable for all kinds of manufacture, and particularly so for bent work and ship building. They have, from an early date in the history of the county, been a very large element in its progress, prosperity and substantial wealth. The saw-mill is met with in every quarter. At this time there are *sixty* saw-mills in operation.

The county is admirably supplied with water. The Salamonie, Wabash and Little River are the principal streams. There is no considerable portion of the county that is not drained and supplied by living streams. Fine qualities of lime and building stone are found along the principal water courses. The lime produced from the quarries at Huntington is justly celebrated throughout a very extensive region of the central northwest. It underlies about six square miles of territory, and is practically inexhaustible. It is exceedingly accessible. At no point is it more than two feet until a merchantable quality of stone is reached. It has been sustaining a very considerable population, engaged in its manufacture, for several years. Its development is being prosecuted with vigor and very satisfactory results.

A superior quality of building stone is found at Markle, on the east line of the county; on Little River, near Huntington, and at Antioch, near the west line of the county.

The soil is adapted to the vigorous production of all the grains, seeds, grasses, vegetables and fruit indigenous in this latitude.

The construction of the Wabash and Erie Canal to Huntington, in the summer of 1835, brought in a large number of speculators, who bought extensive tracts and held them on speculation. For many years this was a serious obstacle to the settlement and development of the county. The first canal-boat arrived at Huntington in the evening of the 3d day of July, 1835.

The next public improvement was the construction of the plank road from Huntington to Liberty Mills, on Eel River, a distance of sixteen miles, which was completed in the summer of 1853. It was an exceedingly valuable improvement to the country along its route. It has, however, been abandoned.

The Toledo, Wabash and Western Railroad was completed to Huntington in the fall of 1855, the first locomotive arriving on Thursday evening, November 13th.

In 1856 a plank road was completed from Huntington to Warren, on the Salamonie River, which was vastly valuable to the country through which it passed. It has been re-placed, for the greater part of its course, by a gravel road, constructed two years ago.

Gravel roads are being constructed from Huntington to Mt. Etna, on the Salamonie River, a distance of ten miles: from Huntington to Lancaster, on the Salamonie River, a distance of ten miles; and from Antioch to Monument City, a distance of six miles. Other roads of a like character are being contemplated in various parts of the county.

The population of the county in 1840 was 1,579: in 1850 it was 7,850: in 1860 it was 14,867: in 1870 it was 19,036, and at the present time it is not far from 25,000.

The area of improved lands was as follows: In 1836, 1,465 acres: in 1850, 26,703 acres: in 1860, 62,394 acres, and in 1870, 105,453 acres.

The value of lands and improvements and town lots in 1836 was $26,450; in 1850, $908,669: in 1860, $3,405,861, and in

1870, $7,573,192. The value of agricultural implements and machinery in 1850 was $48,013; in 1860, $104,255, and in 1870, $219,095.

The number of horses in 1850 was 1,967; in 1860, 3,913; in 1870, 5,902, and in 1876, 7,070.

The number of cattle in 1850 was 4,769; in 1860, 9,350; in 1870, 10,676, and in 1876, 15,542.

The number of sheep in 1850 was 4,316; in 1860, 12,237; in 1870, 21,058, and in 1876, 16,013.

The number of hogs in 1850 was 11,289; in 1860, 25,137, and in 1870, 20,565.

The value of live stock in 1850 was $42,611; in 1860, $443,867, and in 1870, $832,861.

The value of slaughtered animals in 1850 was $30,147; in 1860, $68,953, and in 1870, $219,508.

The following is the number of bushels of wheat, corn and potatoes produced in the years given :

	1850.	1860.	1870.	1875.
Wheat	76,750	167,225	367,521	318,823
Corn	216,173	539,561	288,840	1,124,498
Potatoes	19,757	6,417	42,655	60,195

Total value of taxables as returned for taxation in 1840 was $109,049, and in 1875, $7,504,470.

The number of churches in 1850 was 6; accommodations, 2,200; value of property, $2,300. In 1860 the number was 24; accommodations, 7,850; value of property, $18,450, and in 1870 the number was 27; accommodations, 9,750; value of property, $130,500.

The whole number of school children enumerated is 7,479. There are 116 schools and 124 teachers in the county. The number of students enrolled in the public schools is 4,800. This does not include the parochial, or other than the common schools of the county, in which about 400 are enrolled. The total revenue for tuition for the last year was $25,934.46, making the average cost of each pupil about $5.40. Teachers are paid from $1.70 to $2.10 per day. During the last year the schools were in session 101 days. The value of school property is $107,600.

The following is an exhibit of the manufacturing interests:

	1860.	1870.
Number of establishments.	57	166
Capital invested	$160,550	$451,710
Number of persons employed.	181	653
Annual cost of labor	$53.592	$132,283
Annual cost of material	$215.613	$453.941
Annual value of products	$350.858	$813,255

In 1870 there were 18 water-wheels, propelling 286 horse-power, and 51 steam engines, propelling 1,271 horse-power, making 1,557 horse-power in machinery in the county. There are fifteen flouring-mills in operation in the county.

Many other statistics are at hand to show the development of the resources of the county. These, however, are thought to be sufficient to give a good practical knowledge of the subject.

Pauperism and crime have always been at a very low per cent. of the population. General intelligence and morality have always characterized the people of the county.

The population is composed of emigrants from many of the States of the Union and several countries of Europe, who have become identified with each other in all the elements of peace, happiness and prosperity, and now presents a homogeneous mass of people who will do good to the stranger and emigrant in their midst.

www.ingramcontent.com/pod-product-compliance
Lightning Source LLC
Chambersburg PA
CBHW031814090426
42739CB00008B/1270